Record of Oral Language
and
Biks and Gutches

Marie M. Clay, Malcolm Gill, Ted Glynn, Tony McNaughton, Keith Salmon

Illustrations by Sandra Wagstaff

Heinemann

Published by Heinemann Education, a division of Reed Publishing
(NZ) Ltd, 39 Rawene Rd, Birkenhead, Auckland.
Website www.reed.co.nz. Associated companies, branches and
representatives throughout the world.

ISBN 0 86863 269 4
SBN 435 80231 3

© 1983 M. M. Clay et al
Record of Oral Language was first published in 1976
by New Zealand Educational Institute.
First published in this edition 1983.
Reprinted 1989, 1991, 1993, 1996, 1997, 1998, 1999 (twice), 2000, 2001, 2002 (twice), 2003

Printed in Hong Kong

Contents

Preface

This volume describes techniques for observing two aspects of language development. The techniques were developed for research studies of three ethnic groups in New Zealand. Experience has shown, however, that both techniques can assist the practising teacher to observe and understand changes in children's language. The present volume is directed towards teachers who wish to do this.

Use of these techniques can help teachers to sharpen their skill in observing what children say, and in collecting accurate and objective records of this. In the first task the child is asked to repeat a set of sentences which are graded for difficulty. In the second the child supplies the missing words in a series of illustrated short stories. Students of linguistics who are trained to attend to matters like linguistic structures and morphological rules would recognise that the language forms used in these tasks come from linguistic descriptions of English. It is not necessary for other observers to understand these linguistic descriptions before using the techniques in order to become sensitive to the nature of a particular child's use of English.

Young children's control of English is assumed to increase gradually over most of their school years. The changes occurring can be monitored through the use of both the techniques described in this volume. From scores teachers could judge which children in a programme had made poor, average or good progress in these two aspects of development. The stage of development for which these techniques are appropriate are

* four to seven years of age for children with English as a mother tongue and
* up to five years after children begin to learn English as a second language.

Performance on these tasks can be used to select children for more intensive attention to oral language learning or to check whether any change has occurred in children's language as a result of a programme. Change over time can be an important indicator of how to learn more about language for themselves.

These techniques have been developed and tested as normative, standardised tests. The difficulty of the items, the reliability of the total scores, the sampling of language behaviours, the suitability of the tasks for the age-group concerned were each carefully assessed. There is evidence of this in the research reports and the technical appendices. However the authors decided against publishing normative scores although these were available on satisfactory samples of urban New Zealand children. One reason was that despite remarkable consistency in the difficulty level of the sentences in the Record of Oral Language it was suspected that scores could vary markedly from one group of children to another depending on their previous opportunities to learn the language. Instead of normative scores it is suggested that any particular school or group keep a record of the range of scores gained by children in that school, and work out the averages for their own groups. This approach places the emphasis where we believe it should be, on teacher observation and child development rather than on the child 'passing' and 'failing'.

Biks and Gutches has not been published before but this is the second edition of the *Record of Oral Language*. Since it first became available it has been used in different ways in South Australia, Queensland, U.S.A., Liverpool, Glasgow and Edinburgh. With only minor alterations to one or two words it can be used in other countries where English is spoken without losing its measurement qualities. Because the items have been carefully assessed by the appropriate statistical techniques used in standardised tests it has been clearly established that the sequence of item difficulty is surprisingly stable across very different groups of children. Research studies have shown that this assessment of oral language discriminates well among children in the United States who are five to seven years of age and have English as a mother tongue (Day and Day, 1979) and is also sensitive to the assessment of changes in the language control for Fijian children who are learning English as a second language (Elley, 1980).

It has been pleasing to note that groups of teachers working on inservice courses or curriculum development projects have been able to use the techniques as a guide to designing and evaluating their language teaching programmes. The techniques have also been used in New Zealand to train teachers and others in observing and monitoring changes in the language learning of non-English-speaking children, following an introductory period in special English language classes.

Part One

Record of Oral Language (R O L)

Using the R O L

The *Record of Oral Language* is to assist teachers to:
- observe aspects of a child's control over oral language
- assess a child's ability to handle selected grammatical structures.

There are two instruments for compiling this record:
- Levels Sentences arranged in three broad levels of difficulty and with two examples of seven different sentence types at each level.
- Diagnostic Sentences providing a more comprehensive exploration of a child's control of language structures.

Details from these two instruments may be used to:
- objectively observe and record changes in a child's control of particular grammatical structures
- group children for specific teaching
- guide a teacher's own use of grammatical structures with individuals in a class.
- assist a teacher to develop a child's control over aspects of language in a systematic way.

It is suggested that teachers first read the Introduction and Chapter 1. Then read Chapters 2-6, paying particular attention to the administration procedure. Practise administering the record to a few children. Accuracy and naturalness of presentation and accuracy of scoring could be checked by tape recording these trial runs. Suggestions for applications of the results of the record are given in Chapter 3. As each group of children is different, teachers will develop their own ways of using the information gained from using the record.

Chapter 7 is not essential reading for administering the record but it provides additional information which will prove useful to many teachers using the Record of Oral Language, particularly in generating sentences for classroom use.

Chapter 8 provides technical information on the construction and development of the record.

Introduction

Why the concern about oral language?

Proficiency in oral language has long been considered important for self-expression and for communicating ideas. Morning talks, news and discussion sessions are familiar ways of encouraging children to reflect on their experience and to share their experience with others.

Educational psychologists like Jerome S. Bruner (1966) stress proficiency in oral language because they regard it as a vital tool for thought. They would claim that without a fluent and structured oral language, children will find it very difficult to think abstractly and symbolically.

Particular attention is now being given to oral language in circumstances where the language or dialect a child uses in the home is different from the one the teacher uses in the classroom. It is considered to be important both socially and educationally that children have an opportunity to learn more about their own language when their mother tongue is different from English. To this end, teachers need to know something of the different languages and different cultures of special groups of children. However, New Zealand teachers also have the responsibility to encourage children to improve their skills in the use of the English language. Teachers therefore need to know something about the structure of the English language and how this structure is acquired by young children. This is as important as knowing about the different languages and cultures of the children they are teaching.

To date teachers have not had available procedures to help them make objective assessments of changes in a child's oral language over time, nor have they been able to make objective appraisal of the oral language of different children. Any assessments that have been made have been based on teacher perception and judgment of rather gross qualities like 'style of delivery' or 'fluency', or alternatively, on tests of articulation and word knowledge.

A survey conducted in Auckland, (Eillebrecht, 1971) asked teachers what they considered to be their greatest needs in teaching language. A simple method of testing children's levels of language performance was the second most popular request in a list of 14 expressed needs.

The Record of Oral Language has been developed in response to that need. However, it is not designed as a test in the usual sense of the word. It is intended to provide teachers with an instrument which they can use in a variety of ways.

In this Record of Oral Language, sentence repetition procedures are used to give insight into ways young children master the different structures found in English sentences. These procedures were derived from research studies such as those of Menyuk (1969); Graham (1968); Clay

(1971). They provide the teacher with a way of describing the most advanced structural level of oral language which a child might listen to with full understanding. By using these procedures a teacher can observe what developments have taken place in a child's control of some language structures from one time to another. The teacher might use the Record of Oral Language to assess change in oral language resulting from a special oral language programme, or simply from a child being in an environment where English is spoken. Results from use of the record could also provide a basis for selection of children whose language development requires special attention.

Why use sentence repetition to measure oral language?

One way to find out how much of the structure of adult speech a child has learned is to ask him to listen to a sentence and to repeat it. By having a child repeat sentences which represent a range of different syntactic structures in English a teacher can learn as much in a relatively short time about his control of those structures as would be learned from listening to the child's spontaneous speech over a much longer period.

There is growing evidence that it is very difficult for a teacher to assess a child's language control in a satisfactory manner on the basis of unstructured classroom observation alone. With time-consuming recording and analysis of large samples of a child's speech it is possible to describe the structures the child can produce. But research has shown that when we analyse a child's attempts to repeat a carefully constructed set of sentences we discover also those grammatical structures which he may be just beginning to understand but may not yet use in normal speech. Hence a child's ability to repeat sentences can give a more generous assessment of his ability to handle grammatical structure than is given by the language he himself produces.

The sentence repetition techniques are not used merely to record the items a child gets right or wrong. Valuable information about a child's oral language can also be gathered from observing what he does with a sentence when asked to repeat one that is too difficult. He may simply omit phrases, words or parts of words. He may substitute phrases, words or parts of words. He may expand the sentence by adding phrases or words. Sometimes he may transpose some parts of a sentence. An analysis of the responses a child gives to a set of sentences carefully ordered for difficulty yields a detailed description of his control over oral language. When a child fails, he usually repeats the difficult sentence in a way which indicates the structures over which he has control.

By using the R O L sentences and making a careful record of children's attempts at repetition a teacher has an objective means of describing changes in children's oral language.

Why does the R O L emphasise structure in language?

In everyday language, to paraphrase Lewis Carroll, we generally say what we mean and mean what we say. What we say (meaning) and how we say it (structure) are not always clearly distinguished. The how of saying things is patterned or structured by rules. These rules make what is said comprehensible. We may acquire the ability to use rules of structure before, or without, being aware of what they are.

A child who says 'I goed to town yesterday' appears to be applying a simple rule he has deduced from listening to others: namely if you mean something happened in the past, you add '-ed' to the simple form of the verb. The English language is more complicated than that, but despite such irregularities the structure of the language used can provide information concerning the meaning of sentences.

It is possible to learn something even from a sentence as apparently nonsensical as:

A brom tribbed and wraggled the shoudy fline.

We can assume that 'a brom' did some 'tribbing and wraggling' and that the 'brom' did it to 'the shoudy fline'. However, when the same words are re-arranged as 'shoudy and tribbed brom fline a wraggled the', the structure does not provide the same clues to meaning.

Structure entails the classification of words or symbols into groups of different syntactic classes. Consider the following sentences —

John and Jane felt tired and angry with each other.
John and Jane felt tired and fought with each other.

By removing the words 'tired and' from the first sentence, an acceptable sentence remains.

John and Jane felt angry with each other.

However, removing the same words from the second sentence leaves only a nonsense sentence.

John and Jane felt fought with each other.

The two sentences differ in structure because 'angry' and 'fought' belong to quite different syntactic classes.

Structure can also be seen as the way in which the meaning of a sentence is in part conveyed by the order of its components. In language the position and order of items play a considerable part in determining meaning. Note the effect of shifting 'not' in this pair of sentences —

Not all those children were given a turn.
All those children were not given a turn.

And compare these two sentences —

John hit Bill.
Bill hit John.

In the sentence —

The doctor gave the mother her baby.

the order of words tells us that it is the doctor that does the giving, the baby that is given, and the mother who gets what is given.

The manner in which words function is another way in which structure affects the meaning of sentences. The sentences —

I promised my mother to sweep the drive.

I told my mother to sweep the drive.

may appear to have the same structure since 'promised' and 'told' belong to the same syntactic class. However, the verbs have different functions, the first implies that 'I' will sweep the drive and the second that 'my mother' will sweep the drive.

If the average speaker did not have a reasonable knowledge of the basic rules of structure, communication would be difficult if not impossible. All speakers employ certain basic rules concerning order of items, classes of items and combinations of classes. Nobody with a good grasp of English is in any doubt as to who does the shooting and who gets shot in —

Bill shot John.

nor would they omit the 'that' from the following sentence —

There's the man that gave the fruit to me.

whereas they would know that it was optional in the following sentence —

There's the man that I gave the fruit to.

The rule governing whether you can leave the 'that' out or not requires the same basic knowledge as is involved in knowing who did the shooting in 'Bill shot John'.

A child who says, 'There's the man what I saw at the shops yesterday, is probably developing skill in using relative clauses; one can hardly expect him to learn all the relative pronouns at once. An attempt to correct this usage could well be interpreted by the child as a criticism of his experimental sentence. A set-back in a child's efforts to develop his oral expression could well curtail his interest in understanding the complex utterances of others. And, after all, the sentence

There's the man what I saw at the shops yesterday.

possibly represents considerable progress in language development over the statement,

See that man there. I saw him at the shops yesterday.

The procedures described in this manual are intended to help teachers to identify the extent of a child's knowledge of basic grammatical structures. To achieve this aim it is important for teachers to recognise steps in the acquisition of language skills so they may assist the process of development from simple forms to more complex ones. A young child is unlikely to understand the fine points of the English language until he has mastered the more common structures.

1 Development of the R O L

The Development of the Levels Sentences and the Diagnostic Sentences.

In 1973 an initial pilot testing and a subsequent full-scale testing programme in Auckland schools examined 5 — 6 year olds' ability to repeat sentences. This research extended the previous work of Clay (1971). The Pilot Programme included particular variants of ten different sentence types so that a total of 369 sentences (see p.39) were included in the initial list.

Detailed analyses of children's success at repeating these sentences led to a careful selection and ordering of 42 sentences which were shown to represent a gradient of difficulty from 'easy' to 'difficult'. The sentences selected were largely restricted to those of simple statement (declarative) form. These sentences constitute the items of the Levels Sentences.

From the other variations of simple sentences (such as negative sentences and sentences with relative clauses) some additional sets of sentences have been included for diagnostic purposes. The Diagnostic Sentences can be used following the administration of the Levels Sentences if a more comprehensive exploration of a child's command of English is desirable.

The Levels Sentences are grouped on the basis of three levels of difficulty. Each level contains two examples of each sentence type and the seven different types are described in the following pages.

The Sentence Types used in the Levels Sentences

Type A: These sentences are composed of a noun phrase *(the subject)* followed by some form of the *verb 'to be'* and some other *simple statement*. They cannot have an object.

Examples:	**Subject**	**Verb 'to be'**	**Simple Statement**
Level 1	My brother's knees	are	dirty.
	The car's radio	was	stolen.
Level 2	That big dog over there	is going to be	my brother's.
	That old truck in there	used to be	my father's.
Level 3	(You)	Be	as quiet as you can when your father's asleep.
	(You)	Be	very careful swimming when there's a big wave.

Note: In Level 3 the Imperative form has been used. In these two sentences a subject (You) is implied.

Type B: These sentences are composed of a noun or noun phrase *(the subject)* followed by a *verb phrase,* followed by a noun phrase which is a *direct object.*

Examples:	**Subject**	**Verb**	**Direct Object**
Level 1	Baby	is drinking	some milk.
	Sally	is riding	her bike.
Level 2	The boy by the pond	was sailing	his boat.
	The cat from next door	was chasing	a bird.
Level 3	My aunt and uncle	want to start building	a new house.
	That dog and the one next door	like to chase	big cars.

Type C: These sentences are composed of a noun or noun phrase *(the subject)* followed by *a verb or verb phrase* followed by one of a variety of *additional constructions* which is not a direct object.

Examples:	**Subject**	**Verb**	**Additional Construction**
Level 1	Sally	is staying	at home.
	Mary	is going	to town.
Level 2	The bird	flew	to the top of the tree.
	The dog	ran	through the hole in the fence.
Level 3•	The two cars	drove	along the road for a long time.
	All the children	talked	loudly to each other at the table.

Type D: These sentences are composed of a noun or noun phrase *(the subject)* followed by *a verb or verb phrase* followed by two noun phrases forming the *indirect* and the *direct objects.*

Examples:	**Subject**	**Verb**	**Indirect Object**	**Direct Object**
Level 1	John	is buying	me	a boat.
	Mary	is giving	me	a book.
Level 2	(For his birthday) Mary	gave	him	a truck.
	(For the holidays) Grandpa	bought	us	a ball.
Level 3	The baker	sold	my father	some hot pies.
	The new teacher	read	our class	a scary story.

Note: The level 2 sentences contain a preposed noun phrase (in brackets) because this proved to be the best item in terms of statistical criteria for the difficulty sequence.

Type E: These sentences are composed of a noun phrase *(the subject)* followed by a *verb* followed by a *noun clause*.

Examples:	Subject	Verb	Noun Clause
Level 1	I	know	he's in there.
	I	guess	we're lost.
Level 2	Can you	see	what is climbing up the wall?
	The boy	saw	what the man was doing to the car.
Level 3	The girl	saw	who her mother was giving the cakes to.
	The teacher	knows	how much wood we will need for the house.

Note: In Level 2 the question form provided the best item in terms of statistical criteria for the difficulty sequence.

Type F: These sentences are composed of *an adverb* (e.g. 'here' or 'there') or *a relative pronoun* (e.g. 'this', 'that', 'these') followed by *a verb* (e.g. 'be', 'come', 'go') followed by the *subject* of the sentence.

Examples:	Adverb or Relative Pronoun	Verb	Subject
Level 1	There	's	another fire engine.
	Here	are	some more fish.
Level 2	Here	comes	a big elephant with children sitting on his back.
	There	is	my baby riding in his push-chair.
Level 3	There	are	the books that you were reading at my place.
	There	goes	the fireman who put out the fire in the building.

Type G: These sentences are composed of a noun phrase *(the subject)*, followed by a *verb or verb phrase*, followed by an *object*, followed by some *additional construction*, (e.g. adverb or adverbial phrase).

Examples:	Subject	Verb Phrase	Object	Additional Construction
Level 1	She	's driving	her car	quickly.
	He	's playing	that music	very loud.
Level 2	My brother	turned	the television	(up) very loud.
	The girl	threw	her book	right across the room.
Level 3	My mother	usually puts	the cat	out of the house at night.
	My brother	often puts	some bread	outside for the birds.

2 Administration

Instructions for administering the Levels Sentences

Each sentence is said by the teacher to the child who then attempts to repeat it. The exact response to each sentence is recorded immediately underneath its sentence for subsequent analysis.

Thus, on the line beneath each sentence on the record form:
(1) Tick each word correctly repeated, and
(2) Write in EVERY deviation from the original sentence
    (even *is* for *'s*).

Examples:

	A1	That big dog over there is going to be my brother's.
Omission		√ √ √ √ √ √ - - - √ √ - .
	C1	The bird flew to the top of the tree.
Substitution		√ √ √ up - - - - - .
Omission		

	D1	For his birthday Mary gave him a truck.
Transposition		√ Mary's √ he √ √ - trucks.
Substitution		
Omission		

	E1	Can you see what is climbing up the wall?
Substitution		
Addition		√ √ √ that thing √ √ √ √ √ ?

	F1	There is my baby riding in his pushchair.
Contraction		
Addition		√ 's a little √ √ √ her pram.
Substitution		

Note: The sentence is scored as correct only if it has been repeated *exactly*.

Accurate recording requires very careful listening. It is easy to predict that the child will give a correct response and assume that is what one heard. Tape recording of administrations provides a check on accuracy.

The R O L presents all the sentences from each level on a separate page. To reduce administration time, teachers should begin with Level 2 as this is the best starting point for most five year old children. However, it is open to the teacher to decide whether children who experience considerable difficulty should begin with Level 1 sentences. In exceptional circumstances where it is apparent that a child is not able to cope with the increasing difficulty of the sentences it is permissible to stop after three failures.

If a child is successful at repeating all the sentences at Level 2 he can be credited with passing all Level 1 sentences. If a child has difficulty with Level 2 sentences then he should be given those at Level 1.

Though it is permissible to begin at Level 1 and proceed to Levels 2 and 3, the administration of the test is shortened by adopting the following recommended administration procedure.[1] (See Fig. 1)

1. The scalability of the Levels Sentences and their difficulty levels enables this procedure to be adopted with confidence (See pages 44 — 46).

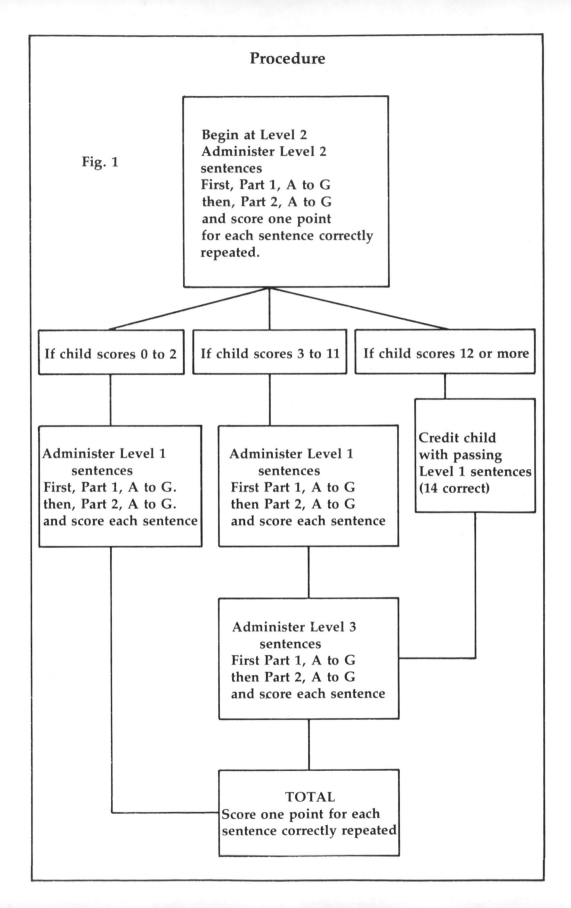

Procedure

Fig. 1

Begin at Level 2
Administer Level 2
sentences
First, Part 1, A to G
then, Part 2, A to G
and score one point
for each sentence correctly
repeated.

| If child scores 0 to 2 | If child scores 3 to 11 | If child scores 12 or more |

Administer Level 1
sentences
First, Part 1, A to G.
then, Part 2, A to G.
and score each sentence

Administer Level 1
sentences
First Part 1, A to G
then Part 2, A to G
and score each sentence

Credit child
with passing
Level 1 sentences
(14 correct)

Administer Level 3
sentences
First Part 1, A to G
then Part 2, A to G
and score each sentence

TOTAL
Score one point for each
sentence correctly repeated

Administration Procedure

1. The record should be administered in a quiet place. It is necessary that the sentences be presented out of the hearing of children who are to be assessed later.

2. Before beginning the administration, spend a few moments in establishing rapport with the child. This can be done while you enter the following information on the Record Form:

   Child's name
   Class
   School
   Child's date of birth (obtain from school register)
   Date of Record
   Name of Recorder.

3. Begin by using the following simple familiarization procedure. Say: "I would like you to say some sentences for me. Here is the first one —
   Say — Tom is running to school.

   _____

   Good. Now say —
   I want Bill to come.

   _____

   Good. Now say —
   What is the time?

   _____

   Now let's try these ones".
   If necessary, teachers can vary the instructions slightly to make sure that children understand what is required of them.

4. Throughout the administration of the sentences, make sure that you have the child's attention before presenting a new sentence. If the child's attention has wandered, wait until you have regained it before carrying on with further sentences. The child encounters two examples of each sentence type at each level. This is to ensure that failure on any one sentence due to momentary lapse of attention will not necessarily result in the child failing both sentences of that type.

5. The phrasing, or grouping of words, has been indicated by italics, but the sentences should be spoken clearly with natural intonation and pace.
   It is permissible for schools or researchers to make copies of the Levels Sentences and Diagnostic Sentences for their own use. These should be set out in the same manner as in this manual. It is essential that when stencils are typed, words which appear in italics in the manual are underlined by the typist. If this is not done it will not be possible to administer the items with the correct phrasing.

Class:..............

Date of Birth:..............

School:..............

Age: ....

Recorder:..............

Child's Name:..............

The Levels Sentences

Level 2 Part 1.
TYPE

A *That big dog over there is going to be my brother's.* ☐

B *The boy by the pond was sailing his boat.* ☐

C *The bird flew to the top of the tree.* ☐

D *For his birthday Mary gave him a truck.* ☐

E *Can you see what is climbing up the wall?* ☐

F *Here comes a big elephant with children sitting on his back.* ☐

G *My brother turned the television up very loud.* ☐

Level 2 Part 2.
Type

A *That old truck in there used to be my father's.* ☐

B *The cat from next door was chasing a bird.* ☐

C *The dog ran through the hole in the fence.* ☐

D *For the holidays Grandpa bought us a ball.* ☐

E *The boy saw what the man was doing to the car.* ☐

F *There is my baby riding in his pushchair.* ☐

G *The girl threw her book right across the room.* ☐

Total for Level 2 ☐

Enter 14 on the next page if all Level is credited.

Level 1 Part 1.

Type

A *My brother's knees are dirty.* ☐

B *Baby is drinking some milk.* ☐

C *Sally is staying at home.* ☐

D *John is buying me a boat.* ☐

E *I know he's in there.* ☐

F *There's another fire engine.* ☐

G *She's driving her car quickly.* ☐

Level 1 Part 2.

Type

A *The car's radio was stolen.* ☐

B *Sally is riding her bike.* ☐

C *Mary is going to town.* ☐

D *Mary is giving me a book.* ☐

E *I guess we're lost.* ☐

F *Here are some more fish.* ☐

G *He's playing that music very very loud.* ☐

Total for Level 1 ☐

Level 3 Part 1.
Type

A *Be as quiet as you can when your father's asleep.* ☐

B *My aunt and uncle want to start building a new house.* ☐

C *The two cars drove along the road for a long time.* ☐

D *The baker sold my father some hot pies.* ☐

E *The girl saw who her mother was giving the cakes to.* ☐

F. *There are the books that you were reading at my place.* ☐

G *My mother usually puts the cat out of the house at night.* ☐

Level 3 Part 2.
Type

A *Be very careful swimming when there's a big wave.* ☐

B *That dog and the one next door like to chase big cars.* ☐

C *All the children talked loudly to each other at the table.* ☐

D *The new teacher read our class a scary story.* ☐

E *The teacher knows how much wood we will need for the house.* ☐

F *There goes the fireman who put out the fire in the building.* ☐

G *My brother often puts some bread outside for the birds.* ☐

Total for Level 3 ☐

Level 1 ☐

Level 2 ☐

Grand Total ☐

The Diagnostic Sentences

The Diagnostic Sentences may be presented in the same manner as the Levels Sentences. They consist of several variations of the simple sentence types i.e.

Imperative sentences
Questions
Negative sentences
Preposed phrases
Relative clauses
Adverbial clauses

They provide a basis for exploring the child's language beyond the Levels Sentences. But they still do not exhaust the variations that can occur in English.

The Diagnostic Sentences are arranged in an order of difficulty experienced by the children in the main study. Each section (e.g. Questions I) represents a steep gradient of difficulty.[1] Suggestions for the use of Diagnostic and Level Sentences follow on page 29.

Note: The teacher may say either 'who' or 'whom' in numbers 63 and 73. Either response by the child is scored as correct.

---

1. See Technical Section (Page 45). It will be noticed that there are variations from the difficulty gradient in a few places. The sentences in Set 1 were arranged in difficulty order, but Set 2 was formed from sentences which matched those in Set 1 and fulfilled the statistical requirements for items.

Imperatives — I

Item

1 *Come and watch him climbing the tree.* ☐

2 *Go and play with your brother in the garden for a while.* ☐

3 *Go to the doctor's with your sister now!* ☐

4 *Hang John's coat on the hook for him.* ☐

5 *Hurry and get the children a few crayons.* ☐

Imperatives — II

Item

6 *Fix my shirt and pants please.* ☐

7 *Go and look for your bag in the kitchen after dinner.* ☐

8 *Ask for some apples at the shop, then.* ☐

9 *Shine the torch on the steps for the visitor.* ☐

10 *Run and find the milkman two more bottles.* ☐

Questions — I

11 Are you selling him your bike? ☐

12 Did you watch the man lighting the fire? ☐

13 He won't lose my puppy dog, will he? ☐

14 Can I play with Jane at her house, now? ☐

15 Where did the lady try to hide her money? ☐

16 Is the truck by the gate red or green? ☐

17 The old man isn't very good at swimming, is he? ☐

18 Can the driver see the cars alright in the dark? ☐

19 What kind of fruit will we buy to make some jam? ☐

20 Did any of the birds eat the bread you fed them? ☐

Questions — II

21 Are you lending him your pencil? ☐

22 Did the teacher see the boy chasing me? ☐

23 They've gone, haven't they? ☐

24 Are we going to Grandma's for lunch tomorrow? ☐

25 What did the boy want to make for his brother? ☐

26 Is the cup in your hand full or empty? ☐

27 Most boys and girls like swimming, don't they? ☐

28 Did you see the policeman last night chasing robbers on his bike? ☐

29 How much of this wood will we need to build a boat? ☐

30 Did any of the children catch the lollies he threw? ☐

25

Negatives — I

31 Most cows can't eat short grass. □

32 Mary's teacher didn't give her a tick. □

33 Don't be so nasty to your little brother. □

34 John's book isn't in his bag any more. □

35 The bird can't fly very far in the rain. □

36 The girl didn't find any milk in the fridge for the baby. □

37 The ladies didn't want to stay outside in the rain. □

38 That car over there isn't really your brother's is it? □

Negatives — II

39 Some people can't drink strong tea. □

40 Peter's father wouldn't get him a school bag. □

41 Don't be so careless with that sharp knife. □

42 Peter's father isn't home from work yet. □

43 The boy didn't want to climb very high up the ladder. □

44 He didn't move his car far enough off the road. □

45 (No satisfactory item) □

46 The policeman in the car isn't really your father, is he? □

Phrases — I

47 On Saturday the boy is going to the circus. ☐

48 At the hospital the nurses saw the doctor. ☐

49 The lady stopped playing the piano to listen to the children. ☐

50 In a minute we'll go and look for him in the garden. ☐

51 Last weekend his father made him a sailing boat. ☐

52 On Monday John took his puppy to school with him. ☐

53 In the nest there were three baby birds. ☐

Phrases — II

54 In a minute we'll play in the sandpit. ☐

55 On television the children watched 'Play School'. ☐

56 The boys let ten balls roll slowly down the hill. ☐

57 This year we're going to a farm for the holidays. ☐

58 On Saturday Aunty brought us a box of chocolates. ☐

59 On the way to school we watched some men digging a hole in the road. ☐

60 Under the car there were two black cats. ☐

Clauses — I

61 *John's in bed* because he's been sick. ☐

62 *I threw him the ball* because he asked me to. ☐

63 *The man who(m) I met* was mowing the lawn. ☐

64 *I gave Linda the book* she showed you. ☐

65 *If his father isn't home* the boy will be sad. ☐

66 *I want some bread* for the bird I found outside. ☐

67 *After he had his breakfast* the boy brushed his teeth. ☐

68 *Jane's playing with the girl* who lives next door. ☐

69 *If the cat climbs on the roof* the birds will fly away again. ☐

70 *While you mind my bike for me* I'll take my bag inside. ☐

71 *This is the chocolate* that was in my bag. ☐

Clauses — II

72 *Jane's at home* because it's a holiday. ☐

73 *He thanked me very much* when I gave him the ball. ☐

74 *The girl who(m) we passed* was wearing boots. ☐

75 *Bill showed me the bike* you sent him. ☐

76 *When the room is tidy* we will be ready for our story. ☐

77 *I asked John for the ball* I threw to him. ☐

78 *If the stone has broken the window* my father will make me fix it. ☐

79 *Bill's looking for a bike* that goes very fast. ☐

80 *When my friends came to my place* we played outside all afternoon. ☐

81 *When the man put the box on the table* he knocked a cup on the floor. ☐

82 *That is the book* that was on the table. ☐

3 Application

The Diagnostic and Level Sentences can be used in a number of different ways and for a range of circumstances. Teachers will develop ways of applying the Record of Oral Language and its findings to suit the needs of their particular class or school.

If, for example, a child is heard using a negative sentence in an unusual way his teacher might wish to use BOTH the Levels Sentences AND the Diagnostic Sentences to explore this problem. She might find out what types of simple sentences the child can and cannot control in the Levels Sentences. Then, turning to the Negative Sentences in the Diagnostic Sentences, she could check the child's ability to repeat Negatives -I. When he has failed three items consecutively she could give the child a second chance on the parallel item types in Negatives -II. After 3 failed items it is good practice to discontinue testing as further success is unlikely. From this information the teacher will know more precisely than she did before about the structures that are causing problems and about the content to use in remedial exercises.

The Selection of Children Needing Special Attention

A useful procedure for a teacher to follow with children in their first year of instruction would be to form a group comprised of the lowest scoring third of her class on the Levels Test and give these children extra time and enriching activities in oral language. Although it is time-consuming to administer the R O L to the whole class it is unwise for teachers to rely on just the evidence of their unstructured observations or their intuitive feelings in deciding which children are in the lowest third of the class.

In general, children scoring below 13 will so far have acquired only a limited control over the structures of oral English.[1] They will be likely to have difficulty in following all but the simplest form of instructions given by the teacher and in following a story read to the class. These children should be considered for special attention in oral language development. Children with a hearing loss may also have low R O L performance.

Guidelines for Action
Provide a competent adult model
The most effective way of raising the level of a child's control over the structures of English is to provide him with many opportunities to speak with a competent and flexible adult speaker of English. This competent adult speaker should be able to:

- speak English accurately and fluently
- get to know the child's particular interests and enthusiasms
- get to know what particular words and expressions mean for particular children
- share ideas and experiences with the child using sentences only a little more complex than the ones the child is using.

1. They will be more than one standard deviation below the average score for our normative sample.

Assistance with this very important aspect of oral language development could be provided by teachers' college students during their periods of being assigned to a class or by teacher aides and mother helpers. The critical qualification is being able to talk *with* a child.

Analyse the record

Study the details of the way in which a child has attacked the Level Sentences which proved too difficult for him to repeat correctly. Look for any patterning of errors. Try to establish what he does when he repeats difficult sentences. Does he omit words, substitute words or expand the sentences? Do these changes occur with particular types of sentences? Is there any information which could account for a particular kind of error? For example, does he come from a home where another meaning is given to a word or phrase used in the R O L sentence? Could the difficulty be accounted for in terms of a specific vocabulary difference, which renders the sentence more difficult than intended? To check this out, try a number of sentences, identical, in structure but employing other words.

Adjust the classroom language

Identify the types of sentences the child is able to repeat correctly, and use these as a guide for checking the level of language used with the child in any aspect of his classwork.

Begin at the level of sentences the child can handle

The starting point for individual oral language work with each child will be the experiences a child wants to talk about. But this may provide the teacher with an opportunity to encourage the development of the child's control of sentence patterns, as well. For this structural aspect of his language programme the child should begin with sentence types that he can repeat without error. The basis of any individual work is the provision of plenty of conversation with an adult using sentences at this level, which the child can easily control. There should be no urgency to hurry the child on to more difficult sentences. On the other hand the programme must have the spontaneity and naturalness of conversation. Confining the programme to repetitive exercises around these sentences the child knows would be unduly restrictive.

Select sentences for special attention

Locate a sentence in the Level or Diagnostic Sentences which closely resembles the level of competence of some children whose language needs extending. The R O L sentences themselves must not be used as practice items. Identify the type of sentence involved and use more sentences of the same structure in oral language exercises.

If, for example, a child has difficulty with a Level 2 form then try him with Level 1 prior to eventually moving back to Level 2. If he is comfortable with a Level 2 form then he may be tried out on Level 3.

It should be noted that there are *two* gradients of difficulty in the Level Sentences. The first of these is to be found *within each level*. Sentences are arranged so that the easier ones are placed earlier in each group of Levels Sentences. Thus Type A sentences are generally easier than Type B, and Type F are easier than Type G.

The second gradient of difficulty is *within each sentence type*. In general, Level 1 examples of sentence types are easier than Level 2 sentences. A child who is successful on sentence Types A, B and C at Level 1 might progress towards understanding more elaborate examples like those of similar type which are illustrated by Level 2 sentences.

Generating Practice Sentences

The type descriptions (see pp 13—15) provide a guide for writing practice sentences of the required type. The information in Chapter 7 gives further details of the sentence structures and pages 39—40 of Chapter 8 may be of assistance in understanding the linguistic factors involved in controlling the nature and difficulty of sentences.

A guide to simplifying or complicating a sentence type will be found by comparing the items from Levels 1, 2 and 3 for that type (pp 13—15).

As an example, new Type B sentences could be written by substituting appropriately in the item sentences —

		Subject	Verb	Direct Object
Level 1	Item:	Baby	is drinking	some milk.
	Exercise:	Mary	is waving	a flag.
Level 2	Item:	The boy by the pond	was sailing	his boat.
	Exercise:	The girl with the hat	was bouncing	her ball.
Level 3	Item:	My aunt and uncle	want to start building	a new house.
	Exercise:	The doctor and his wife	need to lose	some weight.

Substitutions of this kind will not automatically generate sentences of suitable difficulty. The factors which influence difficulty are very complex. However, as teachers gain experience in writing sentences of a given type, and especially of using those sentences with children, they should find the writing easier. It should also become more likely that the sentences written are of appropriate difficulty.

Introduce more difficult sentences in a systematic manner

a. By studying the structures in the Levels Sentences and in the Diagnostic Sentences, teachers will become more sensitive to the problems confronting the child when *too many* difficulties are introduced to him simultaneously. This can occur when a teacher does not consider the level of oral language that is used in the classroom. Children can handle imperative sentences and short declarative sentences with relative ease. Therefore, in the early stages of a language programme it is wise for the teacher to limit the number of words, phrases, clauses and embellishments that are used and encourage flexibility in pupils in the use of a variety of forms of simple structures.

b. Introduce a new feature (e.g. the indirect object) in a sentence based on familiar structures so that the new feature is the only difficulty. Thus:

familiar structure: John is buying a boat.
new feature introduced: John is buying *me* a boat.

Use rhythm, intonation and meaning to direct attention to that feature.

c. The sentences in the diagnostic section provide systematic variations on the simple statement forms used in the Levels Sentences. Moreover, it is unusual to find that —

Imperative sentences are easy.
Questions are relatively easy.
Negative sentences are fairly difficult.
Preposed phrases lengthen and complicate a sentence.
Adverbial clauses further increase the difficulty.
Relative clauses are difficult.

Therefore the diagnostic sentences provide a source of items of varying complexity, from which appropriate selections should be made to suit the particular needs of a child.

Check on progress

Use the Level Sentences to check on a child's progress over time. You may want to discover how many more structures he can handle after he has spent some time in a special oral language programme, or merely after he has spent some time in the general classroom situation. Is your programme making any noticeable difference? The Record of Oral Language may be administered at intervals of six months. Alternate halves can be formed by using just Part 1 or just Part 2 of each Level or of the Diagnostic Sentences. These alternate halves can be administered at three month intervals. e.g. Part 2 three months after using Part 1.

4 Relationship to Other Programmes

In the Department of Education publication, *Language Programmes For Maori Children*, (1972) teachers are asked to 'identify your pupils' strengths — that is, what they already know and what they can already do. This tells you what they are ready to learn, and so determines your starting points.' (p.15) The R O L is designed to be an aid in this identification of strengths, and it will also suggest some of the content to be built into the four interacting approaches to teaching language suggested in the Department's publication (pp23 — 203). The most obvious application of insights from the R O L of a child's control of English would be in the section on Repetitive Practice (pp177-194) but discerning teachers will see that knowledge of the nature of that control will be relevant to any of the four interacting approaches recommended.

5 Additional Comments

Other dialects

If a child from an English-speaking home is heard to say:

'Her b'aint a-calling we : us don't belong-a she'.

he is probably speaking the language heard in his home. The school is expected to help the child to learn to read books which might say:

'She isn't calling us : we don't belong to her'.

It is important to note that both statements are examples of rule-guided speech patterns, one of which the child has already acquired. It is not a case of regarding the first sentence as wrong. It is more a case of teaching the child *another* way of saying the same thing, that is, teaching him *another dialect*. A child is greatly helped by the different settings he is in and can grow in his ability to discriminate among them. He will learn to use one type of sentence in one place, and a different type of sentence to say the same thing in another place. One of the teacher's tasks is to encourage this kind of discrimination so that a child can grow in his ability to communicate in the different settings in which he is placed.

Other languages

A school entrant who already speaks another language may score very poorly on the R O L sentences. However, because he is already familiar with a set of rules about ordering of parts of sentences, about restrictions as to what structures can go with what, and about rules of inflection, he can be expected to master similar sets of rules governing the English language. He will begin slowly, but will probably gain momentum through a sequence of learning the more regular, more frequent and simpler structures first, in much the same way as a younger child learns English as his mother tongue.

Other cultures

During the development of the Record of Oral Language there were opportunities to try using it with several groups of children who had different kinds of language experiences up to the age of five years. It was used in Scotland and Liverpool where spoken English is different in some ways from New Zealand English; with both bilingual Chinese and Dutch children in New Zealand, and with monolingual children from these groups; with a large sample of urban Maori children who were monolingual in English; and with children who had language difficulties and were referred for speech therapy. In all these widely different samples the item statistics varied very little. This suggests that the sequence of difficulty which has been obtained for the R O L sentences does not vary much for any of the tested groups. They may score at different *levels* on the Record but their control over the structures of English seems to be achieved in a similar learning order.

6 A Final Word

Children who are learning to speak English catch on to the rules, first by grasping the easy structures, then those of medium difficulty, and finally those of greater difficulty which are usually those of infrequent or irregular usage. These children master the complexity of English without the benefit of formal tuition in how to speak their mother tongue. In the face of such skill with the complex nature of language learning it would be presumptuous for anyone to assume that the R O L sentences can serve as a complete basis for devising a teaching sequence.

However, it is hoped that the R O L sentences will provide the teachers with some appreciation of the need to take into account structural differences in English sentences when they are devising oral language programmes. It is hoped that teachers who are primarily concerned with fostering interest and spontaneity in oral language activities will see advantages for language teaching through objectively recording and assessing changes in children's oral language. Teachers who use the Record of Oral Language to gather insights about children's control of language structures, will be able to develop their own applications of the findings to suit their particular needs.

7 Further Details of the Sentence Structures

This section can be read in conjunction with the sentence type descriptions (pp13—15) and the first three sections of Chapter 8 (pp38—40) to assist teachers in writing sentences for oral language work.

The R O L sentence could not hope to cover exhaustively the great variety of structures found in English. They deal only with the structures that were within the ability and experience of the average child of five years.

Basic Structures Used in the Levels Sentences

The basic structures used in the Levels Sentences may be described as follows:

1. The major sentence types are those containing a verb which is not the verb 'to be' plus a complement or adjunct. The table below demonstrates several different ways of representing the major sentence types. Column 1 is the type label used in the R O L and detailed on pages 13-15. Column 2 is the form used in Clay (1971). This classification is a much simplified way of recording a phrase structure description of the sentence types of English. N stands for a noun phrase, V for all parts of the verb and the plus sign (+) is used for a variety of structures that can occur in that position.

The analysis shown in the final column is based on that used in Scott et al (1968).

		S	P	C		A	
Type B	NVN	Bill	saw		John		SPC^E
Type C	NV+	Bill	went			to town	SPA
Type D	NVNN	Bill	sent	John	a book		SPC^{E}C^I
Type E	NVNclause	Bill	knows		what he wants		SPC^{E}SPC$^E_{(\beta)}$
Type G	NVN+	Bill	sent		John	to town	SPC^{E}A

Key

  S — subject   C — complement
  P — predicator or verb   A — adjunct

Complements are of several forms:

  C^E — extensive. Such complements can be transformed into the subject of a corresponding clause and do not require number concord with S or P
  C^I — intensive. Such complements cannot be transformed into the subject of a corresponding clause and do require number concord with S or P

The (β) in Type E indicates that a dependent clause acts as a word (as the direct object of the verb). Such a clause is 'rank shifted'.

2. The 'N be +' pattern is set apart because the verb "be" has very little in common with other verbs of English.

    Nbe +   That is my book SPC^I

Different elements that can follow the verb to 'be' in what is called an equational sentence are:

an adverb	Bill is *outside.*
a prepositional phrase of place	Bill is *in bed.*
an adjective	Bill is *cold.*
a noun group	Bill was *a shearer.*

3. The *Here is* pattern is unusual since the element (here or there) which precedes the verb is not the 'subject' of the sentence but refers to location.

    There are John and Jane.

When changed to its question form 'There are John and Jane' does not give 'Are there John and Jane?' but it does give

    Are John and Jane there?

This locational use of 'There is' is a structure used in the R O L sentences. It is distinct from the 'existential' use of 'There is' in which 'there' acts as a substitute subject, as in

    There are three sausages.

This does give a question form of

    Are there three sausages?

Some sentences might be interpreted as using either the locational or existential function and depend on context for comprehension. e.g.

> There is a man who is eight feet tall.

The existential use is not employed in the R O L.

Other Structures Used in the R O L

With some sentences in the speech of very young children like

> You like me Mummy.

it is impossible to decide whether the child is

- requesting or demanding (imperative)
- stating that this affection exists (declarative)
- asking whether Mummy likes him or her (question).

It is only by the child responding to the mother's reply that she knows which meaning was intended for the sentence.

As a child's language develops, rules are applied to the basic patterns to produce more complex constructions. The Diagnostic Items provide some such constructions.

1. The *imperative* is simpler in structure. It is like the declarative with a deleted or implicit 'you' subject. Compare the declarative and the imperative forms:

> She scratches herself.
> Scratch yourself.

2. The rules of formation of *questions* are complex. To arrive at the standard form of the question in English the child has to be able to

- Use the declarative form correctly
- Distinguish a verbal element from all the other elements in the sentence
- Transfer this element to the beginning of the sentence in front of the subject.

An example can be taken from the question form of English which demands a 'yes' or a 'no' reply.

You can ride my elephant.	Yes/No
You have broken my walking stick.	Yes/No
You like me.	Yes/No

To form a question the child must identify the verbal group of the sentence and decides whether it contains one of a small group of verbs (can, may, have, be, shall, will) known as auxiliaries. If so, then this item is shifted in front of the subject.

> Can you ride my elephant?

If, however, one of these items is absent, then its function must be filled by do or did e.g.

> You like me.   becomes
> Do you like me?

because one can't say

> Like you me?

Skill in forming these questions implies an intuitive capacity to analyse the sentence into various components of different grammatical status.

3. *Negatives.* To form a negative many young children will tend to insert <u>not</u> or <u>no</u> at apparently haphazard positions in a sentence. For example a child may insert <u>no</u> before the verbs of this sentence:

> Pussy no eat my meat.

or a not at the beginning of the sentence:

> Not pussies allowed to walk on water.

Producing the conventional negative structure requires much the same knowledge as is needed for the question form, identification of auxiliaries, or in the absence of these, insertion of <u>do</u> or <u>did</u>. The <u>not</u> element is inserted immediately after the auxiliary and often collapsed into the forms <u>don't</u>, <u>didn't</u>, <u>can't</u>, <u>isn't</u>, etc.

4. *Tag Questions* require a combination of the knowledge used for both negative and yes/no questions.

	Main clause					**Tag**	
(i)	They	've	gone,	have	n't		they?
(ii)	They	haven't	gone,	have			they?
(iii)	He		went,	did	n't		he?

In (i) an affirmative declarative main clause has been given a negative question tag.

In (ii) a negative declarative main clause has been given an affirmative question tag.

The tag question is (iii) is in a negative form with did inserted. The meaning of tag questions can change according to context.

5. Recognition of certain grammatical classes is also implicit in the ability to produce *statements preceded by adverbial phrases.* A child needs to be able to recognise not just the group of words itself, but also the function of that group of words in these two sentences.

> There were two black cats under the car.
> He fell under a bus.

The prepositional group 'under the car' can be shifted to the beginning of the sentence,

> Under the car there were two black cats.

but shifting 'under a bus' to the front of the sentence produces rather strange English.

6. In the *relative clause* a basic sentence structure is embedded with another to describe or qualify a noun in the host sentence. The relative clause constructions introduce many intricacies.

From two basic sentences

> I met a man.
> He was mowing the lawn.

the relative clause forms a single complex sentence.

Either,   I met a man who was mowing the lawn.
    or,   The man who(m) I met was mowing the lawn.

A number of rules must be observed. The relative pronoun must follow the noun it refers to; only a preposition may separate them. Standard English necessitates a choice between 4 forms according to certain features of the noun to which it refers, (who,   which,   that,   what).

As described below, in adverbial clauses the subject need not be repeated when the verb contains 'is' or 'are' in relative clauses.

I like the girl who is sitting on the wall.
I like the girl .... sitting on the wall.

7. *Adverbial clauses* fill the same function in the sentence as adverbial phrases, and they are equally moveable.

He thanked me very much then.
He thanked me very much when I gave him the milk.
I found a dollar there.
I found a dollar where I'd left my car.

In adverbial clauses the noun (or its pronoun substitute) need not be repeated under certain conditions, such as when the subject is identical in adverbial clauses.

While I was going to school I fell under a bus.
While .... going to school I fell under a bus.

Among the books which would be useful for teachers wishing to know more about the structural linguistic approach to the study of language are those by Scott et al (1968) and by Dale (1972). Both of these are listed in the references on page 48.

8   Technical Information

Construction of Test Items

The items compiled for the pilot study were designed to represent cells in the following matrix of structures.

Transformations								
Type	Basic Structures	Declar-ative	Imper-ative	Yes-No Question	Nega-tive	Preposed Phrase	Relative Clause	Adverbial Clause
A	**Nbe +**							
B	**NVN**							
C	**NV +**							
D	**NVNN**							
G	**NVN +**							

Supplementary sentence types in addition to those in the matrix were

    Here be..

    Wh-questions

    Tag questions

    Multi-predicated clauses

    Noun clauses — 2 sets

Thus there were 35 structures in the matrix and 6 supplementary types giving a total of 41 sets. Each set had 3 levels of difficulty (123 subsets) and each subset contained 3 equivalent examples. This gave 369 items in all.

Origin of the Items

Examples of child utterances were compiled from the literature on language acquisition and from a pilot study. However as very few structures needed in the matrix were well represented, the majority of the items were made up using a frequency list of child vocabulary (Edwards and Gibbon, 1964) and an Australian research study of sentences used by 5 year old children (Harwood, 1959).

The Linguistic Difficulty of the Items

No single linguistic criterion has been devised for predicting reliably the difficulty of sentences. A combination of factors was used in the creation of the item sentences. There are many factors which influence the difficulty of any sentence. An unusual word or ambiguity of meaning could easily cause an increase in difficulty greater than that produced by a change in grammatical structure or an increase in sentence length. The most reliable guide to difficulty is the nature of children's responses.

The following factors were used to control the difficulty of sentences in the R O L and should be borne in mind when creating new examples.

1. *Morpheme Counts* may not provide a reliable guide to the difficulty of encoding and decoding utterances. For example, in

    He is coming   4 morphemes

    I come   2 morphemes

the first sentence has greater frequency in speech and is probably less difficult for the child to repeat than the shorter second one. Also the problems introduced by affixes and by fused morphemes makes a measure of morpheme count very difficult to apply in a systematic way. However, an attempt was made to keep the morpheme count relatively consistent within each level. Where a sentence has a markedly different morpheme count from other sentences of that type or level it is because other factors have affected its difficulty to a greater extent.

2. *Phrase Count.* The number of phrases in a phrase structure description of the basic sentence must vary because that number is determined by the sentence type. For example, the imperatives necessarily do not have a subject phrase. Sometimes a phrase was added (e.g. as a qualifier of a nominal group). Nevertheless the difficulty level of a particular item could be increased by including additional phrases such as a qualifier of a nominal group. Sentence difficulty was varied by such additions.

3. *Difficult Features*. From research reports it was found that children of this age found the following features difficult: words not often used (nurse); words of greater complexity (shopkeeper); contracted forms, infrequent tenses, irregular forms of verb and nouns; complex verbal groups; coordinated groups; final rather than initial placement of adverbial phrases or clauses. To achieve a progression from easy Level 1 examples of a sentence type to Level 2 or 3 examples some of these difficult features were introduced.

4. *Number of Actors*. Equivalence was sought with respect to the number of actors appearing in paired sentences. Compare —

> May I play with Bill at his house?
> May I play with Bill at Jim's house?

In the second sentence 'Jim's' introduces an extra person and thus an extra semantic element to handle.

5. *Ambiguities*. To avoid ambiguities in sentences with two or more actors when pronouns were used, the actors were differentiated by sex. Also sentences were avoided where the syntax could be misinterpreted momentarily during decoding.

> e.g. That lady teacher...
> *teach*   initially classed as a verb
> The footballers
> *ers* /əz/ misinterpreted as 'is'.

6. *Syntactic Structure of Items*. It was the aim that each clause in a multiclause sentence should conform to the structure type. Certain exceptions were allowed in order to produce natural sentences.

Nominal groups serving a syntactic function in two clauses were regarded as fulfilling the qualification for the basic clause type in each clause; the same consideration applied to relative pronouns.

7. *Semantic Acceptability*. The Australian and English word frequency lists used did not guarantee that the high frequency words used would be known to New Zealand children and the only other means of controlling for meaning was to have the sentences checked by two trained infant teachers.

Hence, in summary: if the test items were intended to probe syntactic control then ideally, phonological, morphological, lexical and semantic aspects of the sentences should not increase the sentence difficulty. One approach would be to use only a limited list of words and morphemes. However, there is also the need to gain the child's cooperation and therefore the sentences should maintain a reasonable level of variety and naturalness. Thus, at the stage of item writing, the difficulty of the items was manipulated by:

1. using a detailed matrix of structures,
2. counting morphemes,
3. counting phrases,
4. noting the difficulty of features,
5. avoiding ambiguities,
6. matching clause structures in multi-clause sentences,
7. keeping the meaning as simple as possible, and
8. using high frequency words.

Pilot Study

Sample

The selection of the actual items for the R O L necessitated the administration of the 369 items forming the item pool, to a random sample of children of the types for whom the instrument was intended. Thus, from a sampling frame of the 238 State and Private schools of the Auckland metropolitan area, a random sample of approximately one tenth (24 schools) was selected. This was done with probability of selection being proportional to size, and with replacement. From each of these sample schools, a second stage random sample of 10 children was chosen. The sampling frame within each school was all those children who were between 5.0 and 6.0 years at testing.

Testing Procedure

As 369 items were considered to be too many for any child to be given, a procedure was devised so that no child was given items unnecessarily. No easy items were given to a child who passed the items of average difficulty, and no difficult ones were given to children failing those of average difficulty.

Testers started each sentence structure at a level of average difficulty — specifically at item 4 of the 9 written. Items 5 and 6 of each structure were subsequently presented. But, in order to prevent the possibility of a structure being learned simply through the successive presentation of its items, other structures were used to separate that structure's item trio at that level of difficulty. Where any error occurred on items 4, 5, or 6 of any sentence type, the easier items — namely 1, 2, and 3 — of that structure were given to the child. However, whether or not the easiest items of a pattern were administered, if any of the average difficulty items of that type were responded to correctly, the harder items 7, 8, and 9 were subsequently given. After three consecutive failures on a sentence structure, testing on that structure stopped. For scoring, *any* deviation from the sentence given for repetition was marked as an error. Thus 'I will' for 'I'll', 'on to' for 'on', 'is' for ''s', 'his' for 'its', and so on were all treated as errors.

In standardizing the procedures for the R O L it was necessary to decide on a consistent way of scoring such responses. While the use of either 'is' or ' 's', for example, may indicate that the child has control over the grammatical structure, the statistics for the R O L have been calculated on the basis of the scoring method described, that is, exact repetition. In a trial rescoring analysis allowing both full and contracted forms to be scored as correct the difficulty level of the items changed only minimally.

The sequence of types and variants was designed not only so that items of a structure were separated from each other, but also so that easier forms were interspersed between more difficult ones. Further, similar structures were separated from one another.

Analysis

For each item, the following statistics were calculated:
(i)   the difficulty index
(ii)   a discrimination index, based on top and bottom 27% groups
(iii) the point biserial correlation between that item and the test as a whole.

Further, the sample was split at the median, and the statistics were recalculated separately for the top 50% and bottom 50%.

Selection of the Items

The basic form of the R O L was planned to be of three levels of difficulty. Thus, the difficulty of an item, as demonstrated by the pilot study, was a core concern when its inclusion in the instrument was being considered. However, other criteria also had to be satisfied.

(i)   The R O L had to be of practical use to teachers, and therefore its components had to be ones which separately and together were pertinent to the classroom situation.

(ii) The set of items to be selected for the R O L had to make linguistic sense. That is, there had to be a clear linguistic rationale for the item statistics of the items making up the R O L.

(iii) Each item had to satisfy certain statistical criteria:
      a) It had to be comparatively easy for children who turned out to be above the median on the final instrument and comparatively difficult for those below the median.
      b) It had to discriminate well among the children ranked at the top on the instrument and among those ranked at the bottom end.
      c) It had to measure the same underlying ability as the instrument as a whole measured.
      d) It had to have a difficulty appropriate for the sentence type and consistent with the other items at that level.

The levels sentences deliberately are selected at varying difficulty levels. The difficulty indices range from .15 to .89. There is no overlap in difficulty from level to level in the Field Trial data graphed on page 47.

An examination of the item statistics from the pilot study showed that it was indeed possible to construct a test with three levels of difficulty, *and* satisfy all the above criteria. This was done by using the declarative form of the five basic sentence types, one of the noun clause structures, and the 'here be +' sentences to select a form other than the declarative in order to get satisfactory item statistics. Instead of the declarative form of NVNN structure in the middle difficulty set of items, the one actually used contains a preposed phrase, *For his birthday Kiri gave him a truck*. Similarly, of the more difficult items, the declarative form of an Nbe + item was not suitable according to the statistical criteria, and the imperative form *Be as quiet as you can when your father's asleep* was included.

It was possible to find two items of each structure at each difficulty level which satisfied the criteria, appropriately tempered for the level concerned. Thus, the core of the Levels Sentences consists of two examples of each of seven sentences types at each of three levels of difficulty. That is 42 items constitute the Levels Sentences section of the Record of Oral Language.

There were, however, many other statistically sound items. These then formed the pool of items from which further selection resulted in the construction of the

Diagnostic Sentences. The three groups of levels sentences and the diagnostic sentences used 123 of the original 369 items.

Main Study

Sample

In order to test the instrument generated by the pilot study, and obtain valid item statistics on all 123 items of the test, it was necessary to sample randomly from the Auckland metropolitan schools again, this time using the information gained from the pilot study in regard to (i) mean school size, (ii) variation within schools, (iii) variation between schools, (iv) mean cost to visit a school for testing pupils, and (v) cost of testing a child. When these factors were weighted appropriately using an optimum allocation formula, it was found necessary to test 3 children from each of 131 schools.

As with the pilot study, the 238 state and private schools in the area constituted the sampling frame, and 131 of these were randomly selected, with probability of selection being proportional to size. Each school was returned to the sampling frame after selection. From each of the sample schools a second stage random sample of three 5.0 to 6.0 year olds was taken and tested.

Testing Procedure

The testers visited one school each day. At the beginning of the school day they obtained their random sample of children who were between 5.0 and 6.0 years on that day, and then spent the rest of the day testing them. Each child was called back three or four times in order to have him complete all 123 items of the instrument.

The order of presentation of the items was as follows:
(i)   The Level 2 items
(ii) The Level 1 items
(iii) The Level 3 items
(iv) The easiest Diagnostic items
(v)   The hardest Diagnostic items.

However, within each of the above sets, the sentences were sequenced in the same way as they had been in the pilot study.
That is,
(i)   similar items were separated from one another
(ii) item pairs were separated maximally, and
(iii) easier forms were interspersed between more difficult ones.

Analysis

Using the whole sample, the same basic item analyses as for the pilot study were undertaken. The item statistics were as follows:

Levels Sentences — Item Statistics

Level 1, Part 1 items	A	B	C	D	E	F	G
Difficulty index	.74	.87	.89	.85	.86	.87	.68
Discrimination index	.46	.27	.21	.29	.26	.24	.49
Point biserial correlation	.51	.46	.38	.46	.37	.34	.47

Level 1, Part 2 items	A	B	C	D	E	F	G
Difficulty index	.72	.84	.85	.76	.56	.70	.70
Discrimination index	.52	.31	.27	.45	.31	.46	.51
Point biserial correlation	.53	.47	.42	.50	.26	.46	.55

Level 2, Part 1 items	A	B	C	D	E	F	G
Difficulty index	.52	.50	.51	.63	.52	.48	.63
Discrimination index	.77	.75	.80	.62	.72	.77	.54
Point biserial correlation	.58	.62	.62	.54	.60	.59	.50

Level 2, Part 2 items	A	B	C	D	E	F	G
Difficulty index	.49	.44	.50	.42	.47	.45	.59
Discrimination index	.81	.72	.72	.68	.77	.64	.71
Point biserial correlation	.61	.56	.57	.53	.61	.51	.60

Level 3, Part 1 items	A	B	C	D	E	F	G
Difficulty index	.32	.20	.37	.38	.20	.32	.35
Discrimination index	.61	.39	.70	.66	.37	.59	.69
Point biserial correlation	.52	.46	.57	.55	.46	.52	.58

Level 3, Part 2items	A	B	C	D	E	F	G
Difficulty index	.26	.15	.21	.24	.18	.30	.30
Discrimination index	.52	.30	.41	.42	.35	.59	.54
Point biserial correlation	.51	.40	.45	.44	.42	.49	.51

Further, for the Levels Sentences the following statistics were calculated for this Main Sample:

Mean	22.3
Standard deviation	9.2
Kuder-Richardson 20 reliability coefficient	0.93

Diagnostic Sentences — Item Statistics

Imperatives — 1	1	2	3	4	5
Difficulty index	.71	.62	.59	.59	.51
Discrimination index	.48	.59	.55	.62	.71
Point biserial correlation	.51	.49	.48	.54	.53

Imperatives — 2	6	7	8	9	10
Difficulty index	.63	.43	.53	.46	.44
Discrimination index	.60	.70	.80	.72	.72
Point biserial correlation	.54	.57	.60	.56	.58

Questions — 1	11	12	13	14	15	16	17	18	19	20
Difficulty index	.71	.69	.65	.62	.57	.53	.41	.37	.33	.21
Discrimination index	.56	.53	.60	.59	.66	.73	.82	.70	.59	.40
Point biserial correlation	.60	.52	.59	.52	.58	.62	.65	.56	.53	.44

Questions — 2	21	22	23	24	25	26	27	28	29	30
Difficulty index	.64	.63	.48	.55	.54	.44	.34	.29	.24	.20
Discrimination index	.67	.69	.71	.70	.80	.72	.51	.52	.46	.39
Point biserial correlation	.59	.63	.54	.56	.66	.60	.42	.50	.45	.42

Negatives — 1	31	32	33	34	35	36	37	38
Difficulty index	.67	.65	.64	.62	.59	.50	.49	.35
Discrimination index	.65	.60	.68	.69	.70	.65	.80	.66
Point biserial correlation	.61	.56	.64	.62	.59	.52	.61	.52

Negatives — 2	39	40	41	42	43	44	45[1]	46
Difficulty index	.60	.55	.63	.59	.47	.49	—	.29
Discrimination index	.68	.71	.74	.72	.85	.79	—	.54
Point Biserial correlation	.55	.57	.66	.64	.64	.65	—	.50

[1] No item met the statistical criteria

Phrases — 1	47	48	49	50	51	52	53
Difficulty index	.56	.53	.50	.47	.44	.43	.40
Discrimination index	.76	.67	.78	.63	.74	.70	.66
Point biserial correlation	.65	.53	.61	.48	.50	.55	.53

Phrases — 2	54	55	56	57	58	59	60
Difficulty index	.56	.36	.17	.16	.36	.19	.38
Discrimination index	.50	.43	.31	.32	.65	.38	.67
Point biserial correlation	.41	.39	.42	.35	.52	.42	.56

Clauses — 1	61	62	63	64	65	66	67	68	69	70	71
Difficulty index	.65	.50	.48	.45	.40	.40	.38	.36	.31	.32	.27
Discrimination index	.61	.77	.78	.69	.64	.58	.50	.66	.57	.49	.50
Point biserial correlation	.55	.62	.61	.56	.53	.50	.44	.54	.48	.39	.46

Clauses — 2	72	73	74	75	76	77	78	79	80	81	82
Difficulty index	.63	.44	.21	.39	.30	.38	.30	.34	.23	.27	.21
Discrimination index	.60	.73	.41	.72	.49	.67	.57	.50	.44	.46	.39
Point biserial correlation	.54	.58	.41	.55	.43	.55	.54	.47	.45	.40	.41

Field Trials

Further trials were conducted with the assistance of speech therapists in the Auckland area. Two samples were used. The first consisted of 100 children drawn at random from all 5 year olds while the second was also of 100   5 year olds but was drawn only from children who had been referred for therapy.

Analysis of the item difficulties from these studies confirms that three distinct levels of difficulty have been obtained. This is shown graphically in fig 2. A teacher can therefore start the administration with items from the middle difficulty level. If these are repeated correctly it is unnecessary to administer the sentences from the lower difficulty level. Since all the Level 1 sentences are of lower difficulty than those of Level 2 it can safely be assumed that the child would pass those items also. This saves considerably in administration time.

An additional outcome of the analysis was to establish that the 42 items of the Levels Sentences have a reproducibility coefficient of 0.83. This was established by Guttman Scalogram analysis. With a perfect scale one could say that if item X were repeated successfully by a child, then all the items below it would also be correctly repeated by the child. (Such a scale would have a scalability coefficient of 1.00). The scalability of the R O L items means that very often one would be correct in predicting that a child who has demonstrated competence with grammatical structure X will also be competent with all structures which precede X on the R O L.

The trials using Speech Therapists as recorders are of importance in the development of the R O L. They confirm that the findings obtained under research conditions with one sample and only two recorders can be replicated with different groups of children using many different recorders under field conditions.

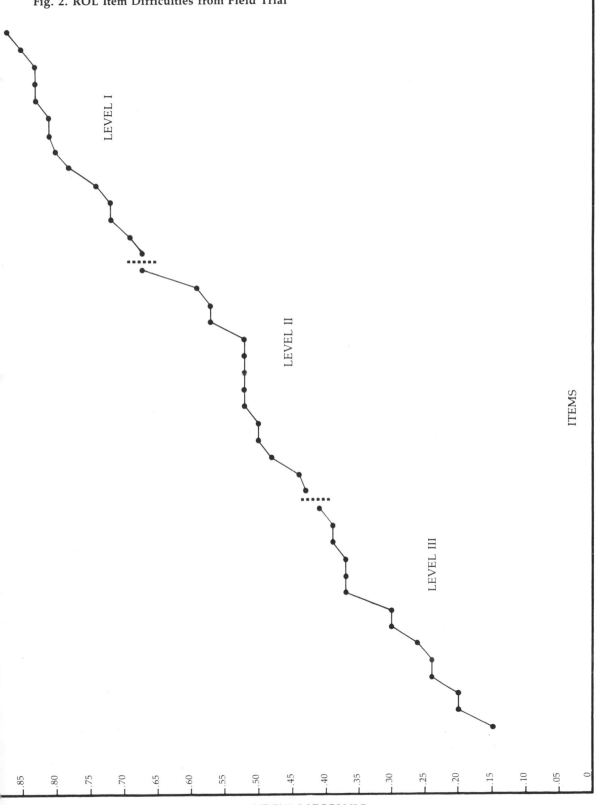

Fig. 2. ROL Item Difficulties from Field Trial

R O L — References

BRINGHAM, T.A. and SHERMAN, J.A. An experimental analysis of verbal imitation in preschool children, *Journal of Applied Behaviour Analysis*. 1968. **1**, 2, 151-158

BRUNER, J., OLVER, ROSE R., GREENFIELD, PATRICIA M. *Studies in Cognitive Growth*, New York: Wiley, 1966

CLAY, MARIE M. Sentence Repetition: Elicited Imitation of a Controlled Set of Syntactic Structures by Four Language Groups. *Monographs of the Society for Research in Child Development* **36**, 3, 1971

DALE, P.S. *Language Development: Structure and Function*. Hinsdale, Illinois: The Dryden Press, 1972

DEPARTMENT OF EDUCATION *Language Programmes for Maori Children*, Wellington 1972

EDWARDS, R.P.A. and GIBBON, V. *Words Your Children Use*, London, Burke, 1964

EILLEBRECHT, B.J. The Teaching of Language: A survey of teacher opinion. Unpublished report, 1971

FRASER, C., BELLUGI, U. and BROWN R.W. Control of grammar in imitation, comprehension and production. *Journal of Verbal Learning and Verbal Behaviour*. **2**, 1963, 121-135

GRAHAM, N.C. Short-term memory and syntactic structure in educationally subnormal children. *Language and Speech*, **1**, 1968, 209-219

HARWOOD, F.W. Quantative study of the speech of Australian children. *Language and Speech*, 1959, **2**, 236-271

JORDAN, CHRISTINA, M. and ROBINSON, W.P. The grammar of working and middle class children using elicited imitations. *Language and Speech*. 1972, **15**, 2, 122-140

MENYUK, PAULA *Sentences Children Use*, Cambridge, Mass.: M.I.T. Press, 1969

OSSER, H., WANG, M.D. and ZAID, F. The young child's ability to imitate and comprehend speech: a comparison of two sub-cultural groups. *Child Development*, **40**, 1969, 1063-1075

SCOTT, F.S., BOWLEY, C.C., BROCKETT, C.S., BROWN, J.G., and GODDARD, P.R. *English Grammar: A linguistic study of its classes and structures*. Auckland: Heinemann Educational Books, 1968

SHERMAN, J.A. Imitation and language development. H.W. Reese (Ed.) *Advances in Child Development and Behaviour*, New York: Academic Press, **6**, 1971

SLOBIN, D.I. and WELSH, C.A. Elicited imitations as a research tool in developmental psycholinguistics (in) C.A. Ferguson and D.I. Slobin (Eds.) *Readings on Child Language Acquisition*, New York, Holt, Rinehart & Winston, 1973

Part Two

Biks and Gutches — Learning to Inflect English Words

Marie M. Clay

Introduction

Questions that can be used to test children's control over the inflections of English are presented here. Some suggestions are made of how teachers might use such an assessment of language acquisition. Two studies are also reported as examples of the way these questions have been used in research.

The young child who has begun to combine words into phrases and sentences uses inflections. He has little difficulty operating as if he had some general notion of the rules that govern word changes (Dale, 1972). He is able to learn a pattern and he applies it as generally as possible, treating irregular examples as if they were regular. He says, *We goed to town,* using a past tense ending which matches *showed* and *mowed.* At times he extends the use of a pattern beyond acceptable limits. At other times he tries to match the patterns around him. There is a steady improvement with the rules for word changes towards mastery of the most difficult at about 12 years (Selby, 1972). The evidence that children's use of inflections is guided by rules was provided by Berko (1958) because her subjects were able to inflect nonsense words in ways which agreed with the inflection rules of English. Kirk and McCarthy (1966) provided statistical evidence from 700 children aged 2:6 to 9:0 that scores on a test of inflections increased regularly with age and were related to many other types of oral language scores.

There is clear evidence from research that the child's control over the inflections of English changes as experience with language accumulates. Simple plurals, possessives and the progressive present tense verbs reach perfect control in the 5:0 to 7:0 year age range. At first children achieve correct performance with the most regular forms which have the fewest variants and only after more experience do they control the irregular and infrequent variants or instances.

A set of questions to test children's control over such rules was designed for a research study. It proved interesting to the adults who observed and the children who participated, and is presented here with some suggestions for how it could be used in educational settings.

What to do with this test

This set of items provides an interesting and informative observation situation. Students and teachers can be sensitised to the differences between children in this aspect of language acquisition. Differences may be observed between children of different ages or between children of the same age who come from language backgrounds that differ markedly.

The items can also be used as a test. For example, it may help teachers to become more aware of the rate and kind of change that is occurring in children's language skill after the introduction of a new or special programme.

For children who have a standard dialect of English as a mother-tongue the test can answer questions like, *Is the child's control over the rules for inflections increasing?* Sometimes this is not the case. Comparison of test and retest scores will allow teachers to observe changes in this particular aspect of language development.

For children who are learning English as a second language the test will show what control the children have gained over inflection skills and some of the things they have yet to learn. It is possible to discover how long they have to be in instruction before they reach the average level of 5:0 — 7:0 year old children with English as their mother-tongue.

For children who speak a dialect of English in which non-standard inflections are the rule, teachers may observe the extent to which the children are gaining control of a standard dialect in addition to the one they already control.

The items were designed for the 5 to 7 year age group and have been used with children up to 10 years.

The choice of items

In selecting items for any measuring instrument in language one has to choose between a comprehensive linguistic survey of all types of instances and a set of selected items which sample only a few items. After a pilot study using many examples with 40 children of mixed ethnic groups a set of 62 items was used in a second pilot study (see Appendix). Thirty-six items were selected from these and they provide a reliable scale. They test the child's capacity to inflect real words. He may have learned each of these real words one by one, and he may not have learned to use the rules for inflections that apply in the English language. This knowledge that there are regular ways of changing words in English enables English speakers to inflect new words they have not learned before. Control over such rules is tested by using nonsense words. If a child inflects a nonsense word correctly he presumably has some sense that *it is done this way in this language*. The nonsense words in this test do not puzzle children, and this is probably because they hear new words all the time in the language around them and treat the nonsense words as new words.

1 Administration

Preparation

It is important that this test be administered in a natural, conversational tone. Rehearse the items until the sentences are familiar. Practise giving the test to several children of different ages and ability to ensure a smooth administration procedure that retains a natural language situation. A tape recording of the administration will often show up problems in the tester's behaviour that a tester does not notice.

Recording

An answer form is provided on page 80. Write in the incorrect responses a child gives, check the correct ones and mark the ones he refused with X.

Administering the items

The child is shown a picture and the tester introduces the items as a story about a picture. For example, showing the picture for items 4, 5 and 6 and pointing to it the tester reads (says):

> The children said to the lady 'Open the door'.
> (*And that's what she's doing.*)
>
> 4 The lady is _____ the door.   (opening)
> 5 But she is careful when she _____ it.   (opens)
> 6 Yesterday she nearly knocked the little girl over,
>   when she _____ the door.   (opened)

Note in the example above that the tester introduced a *minor* variation (in italics) to keep a natural conversational tone. This is allowable.

The tester omits the critical word pausing for the child to say the word. If necessary the tester can lightly articulate the first sound of the response word, 'o_____', to stimulate a child's response. Usually the child will say the word and the tester will complete the sentence, and the story.

In the presentation of nonsense words the child is shown a picture like the one in items 28 and 29. The tester reads:

> 28 This calf knows how to naz. Say 'naz'.
>   What is he doing?
>   He is nazzing.
>   Every day he does this.
>   Every day he _____.   (nazzes)
> 29 Tomorrow he will do it.
>   Tomorrow he _____.   (will naz)

Record the answer given by the child.

What to do with the scores

Results vary from one group of children to another depending upon the characteristics of the language group being tested. For this reason no norms have been provided. Two types of records are recommended.

- **School-based norms** Firstly, it would be a good idea for any particular school or group to keep a record of the range of scores typically attained by the children they work with, and to determine what is high, average and low scoring within that group. Scores change quite rapidly between 5 and 7 years.

- **Change over time** Secondly, the set of items is a useful device for taking a record of one (limited) aspect of language development, and then retesting after a programme has been provided, or a period of time has elapsed, to capture what changes have occurred. Average rates of change for a particular language group could be calculated.

- **Research group means** Mean scores for age groups 5:0 — 7:0 and for age groups 8:0 — 10:0 are found in the Clay (1974) and Presland (1973) studies but standard deviations around those means will probably vary considerably in size from group to group. It is more desirable to devise local norms than to compare scores with these particular research groups.

2 Biks and Gutches items

A record form for an individual child and a cumulative record for building up the range of scores typically found in a class or school are included on pages 80 and 81.

Climb the tree

This boy says, 'Watch me climb the tree.'
What is he doing? Yes, climbing the tree.
He is careful when he climbs.

1 He is a good _____.   (climber)*

(Accept 'boy'; re-adminster, stressing 'cl'.)

The tree house

These boys know how to build a house in a tree.

2 Children like to build lots of _____ in trees.   (houses)

3 The ladder belongs to Father.
   Whose ladder is it?
   It is _____ ladder.   (Father's)

Open the door

The children said to the lady, 'Open the door.'

4 The lady is _____ the door.   (opening)
5 But she is careful when she _____ it.   (opens)
6 Yesterday she nearly knocked the little girl over
   when she _____ the door.   (opened)

Write your name

This boy can write his name on paper.

7 He can write his name all by _____.   (himself)

8 Yesterday he did the same thing. Yesterday he
_____ his name.   (wrote)

9 The boy has this book and this book.
He has two _____.   (books)

10 All the children in this school sit on the floor.
They did the same thing yesterday.
Yesterday they all _____ on the floor.   (sat)

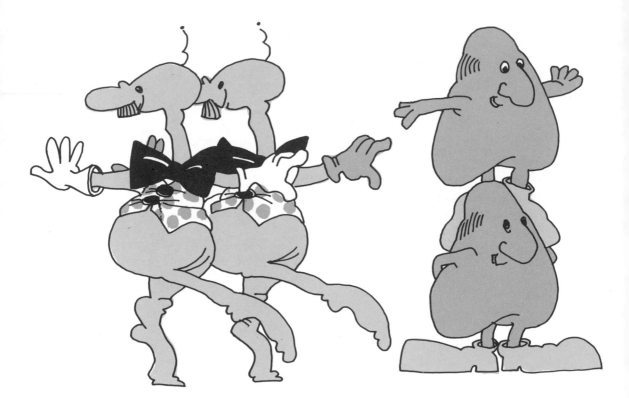

Biks and gutches

11 This is a bik and here is another bik.
   There are two ____. (biks)
12 There is a gutch and here is another gutch.
   There are two _____. (gutches)

Mot the ball

13 The big girl can mot the ball with her foot.
Say 'mot'.
What does she do?
She _____ the ball.   (mots)
14 When the ball rolls very fast she can stop it
with both her *(pointing at both feet)* _____.   (feet)

Wash the car

15 You have to wash a car when it gets dirty.
This lady often does this.
This lady often _____ her car.   (washes)

Paint a picture

16 Peter is painting.

He is happy when he _____.   (paints)

17 Yesterday he did this.

Yesterday he _____.   (painted)

18 I call him a happy little _____.   (painter)*

19 Tomorrow he'll do it again.

Tomorrow he _____.   (will paint)

20 He might paint a wug.

Say 'wug'.

He might even paint two _____.   (wugs)

* (*Accept 'boy'; re-administer*)

Bod the seaweed

21 These boats have been out to gather seaweed.
They have to bod the seaweed into big heaps.
Say 'bod'.
Everyone does this.
This man does this.
This man _____ the seaweed.   (bods)

22 Yesterday they _____ the seaweed on to   (bodded)
boats like this.

23 This man is not _____ his seaweed   (bodding)
into a big heap.

24 They get lots and lots of _____.   (seaweed)

Sweep the street

25 Did you ever see people sweep the street?
All these ladies sweep the streets.
Yesterday they did the same thing.
Yesterday they _____ the streets.   (swept)
26 And tomorrow I think they _____   (will sweep)
the street again.

Calves naz

27 This is a calf and here are lots of _____.   (calves)

28 This calf knows how to naz. Say 'naz'.

What is he doing?

He is nazzing.

Every day he does this.

Every day he _____.   (nazzes)

29 Tomorrow he will do it.

Tomorrow he _____.   (will naz)

Happy people

30 This lady is old.
No-one is as old as her.
She is the _____ one. (oldest)

31 Is the girl as old as the lady?
I think the lady is _____ than the girl. (older)

32 These people have happy faces.
This one is happy. This one is very happy.
And this one is very, very happy.
This last one seems to be the _____ one. (happiest)

33 I think this one is happy but I think
that this one is very happy.
I think this one is _____ than that one. (happier)

Men and guns

34 This is a man and here is another man.
There are two ___.   (men)
35 This man has a gun, and this man has a gun.
They have two ___.   (guns)

36 This man put his gun away and this man
put his gun away.
They both put ___ guns away.   (their)*

(Accept 'the guns' and ask "Whose guns?")

Biks and Gutches

NAME _____ FIRST CHECK   DATE _____   SCORE 1 ____
DATE OF BIRTH _____ SECOND CHECK   DATE _____   SCORE 2 ____
  THIRD CHECK   DATE _____   SCORE 3 ____

		1	2	3			1	2	3
1	climber				19	will paint			
2	houses				20	wugs			
3	Father's				21	bods			
4	opening				22	bodded			
5	opens				23	bodding			
6	opened				24	seaweed			
7	himself				25	swept			
8	wrote				26	will sweep			
9	books				27	calves			
10	sat				28	nazzes			
11	biks				29	will naz			
12	gutches				30	oldest			
13	mots				31	older			
14	feet				32	happiest			
15	washes				33	happier			
16	paints				34	men			
17	painted				35	guns			
18	painter				36	their			

Cumulative Record

SCHOOL, CLASS, GROUP _____

DATE _____

Name	Score	Name	Score

TOTAL SCORES _____ _____

RANGE HIGHEST TO LOWEST _____ _____

MEDIAN OR MIDDLE SCORE _____ _____

MEAN OR AVERAGE SCORE _____ _____

3 Two research studies

Two studies using the items discussed here have looked at changes in the control over inflections of New Zealand children aged 5-10 years. The progress of pakeha (white) New Zealand children with English as their mother-tongue was contrasted with the progress of urban Maori children and urban Samoan children in Auckland.

The children studied were from different language groups. The Optimum English group had a maximum opportunity to learn the rules of English as their parents were professional people with tertiary education and English was their mother-tongue. The Average English children were selected randomly from the available children in the 10 research schools after the Optimum (Professional) group had been removed. The Maori children were unable to score on tests of Maori language, administered by a native speaker, and were monolingual speakers of English (Clay, 1971). The Samoan children had a very limited control of English but most had a fluent command of Samoan for their age (Clay, 1971).

The study was carried out twice, with similar results in both samples. In each sample there were 4 boys and 4 girls at each of the ages 5:0, 5:6, 6:0, 6:6 and 7:0, a total of 40 children in each language group.

A total language score was obtained from four different tests of oral English, namely, articulation, vocabulary, sentence repetition and this test of inflections (Clay, 1970).

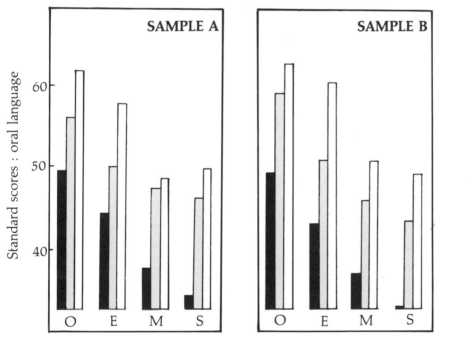

Figure 1: T-scaled scores of four language groups at three age levels on a combined score for tests of oral English [O: Optimum English (Professional parents); E: Average English; M: Maori; S: Samoan].

Combined scores for articulation, vocabulary, inflections and sentence repetition were expressed as T-scaled scores for Samples A and B, and were plotted for all language groups. With only one exception the groups at every age in both Samples A and B were ranked in the order Optimum, Average English, Maori and Samoan (Fig. 1).

On entry to school at 5 years the Optimum group had high language scores which they maintained through 6 and 7 years. The Average English group improved at a similar rate approximately 1 year behind the Optimum group in their control of language. The Maori children who were monolingual in English, were a similar distance behind the Average English group. The bilingual Samoan group had the lowest English language scores at every age tested, with one exception. At 7 years in Sample A the Samoan group exceeded the Maori average which agreed with a claim by teachers that the Samoans do, in time, draw ahead of the Maori children in school achievement but this was not a significant difference in this research and was not supported in Sample B. However, the progress of *both* Polynesian groups at 7 years placed them well above the Average English child at 5 years. The parallel progress of all groups was satisfactory but efforts could be made by schools to accelerate the progress of the Polynesian groups.

An analysis of variance yielded significant main effects for age, and for language groups (p< .001, Table 1).

Table 1 — Analyses of Variance of Language and Age Differences for Samples A and B on a Combined Score for Oral Language

Sample	Source	df	F	P
A	Language	3	31.35	.001
	Age	4	19.95	.001
	L X A	12	0.44	ns
B	Language	3	40.45	.001
	Age	4	24.52	.001
	L X A	12	0.22	ns

The changes in test scores showed that a large amount of language learning was taking place in the first two years of school in each of the four language groups. The rates of progress were similar and parallel. This finding was true of both samples.

On the test of inflections the rate and direction of change followed the general pattern above. The analyses of variance for Samples A and B showed that the language groups and the age groups were significantly different in performance on this test of inflections(p<.001, Table 2).It should be noted that the age group results refer to groups only six months apart, pointing up the rapid change in language skill which takes place at these ages. The differences between language groups were of greater magnitude.

Table 2 — Analyses of Variance of Language and Age Differences for Samples A and B on the Inflection Test Scores

Sample	Source	df	F	p
A	Language	3	41.77	.001
	Age	4	18.07	.001
	L X A	12	0.89	ns
B	Language	3	54.57	.001
	Age	4	18.33	.001
	L X A	12	0.58	ns

The rate and direction of change in the tests of inflections were similar to those of tests of other aspects of language acquisition. The language groups at each age level were in the same order as that discussed above for the Total Language Score. This is shown in Figure 2 in comparison with the three other language tests.

No table has been constructed for the Optimum English Group because the sequence of acquisition or relative difficulty of the items duplicates, with only minor exceptions, that of the Average English Group. Error scores were much lower.

For the urban Maori group it could be hypothesised from socio-linguistic studies that these children learn a Maori/English dialect from their parents. Such a dialect might have its own rules for signalling the meaning changes equivalent to those tested in this research. It is an observation of teachers that Maori children seem to use the inflections of English in flexible ways rather than be constrained by the restriction rules of English morphology. If the dialect hypothesis were valid one might expect to find systematic differences in the error patterns of urban Maori children when compared with children speaking a standard dialect. If what the teachers are reporting is a more haphazard phenomenon then one might expect to find unsystematic differences in the two groups.

Neither of these positions was indicated by the results. The urban Maori group made higher error scores and there were slight variations in the order of difficulty (particularly for irregular plurals and the /əz/ phoneme group) but on the whole Table 4 duplicates the sequence reported in Table 3.

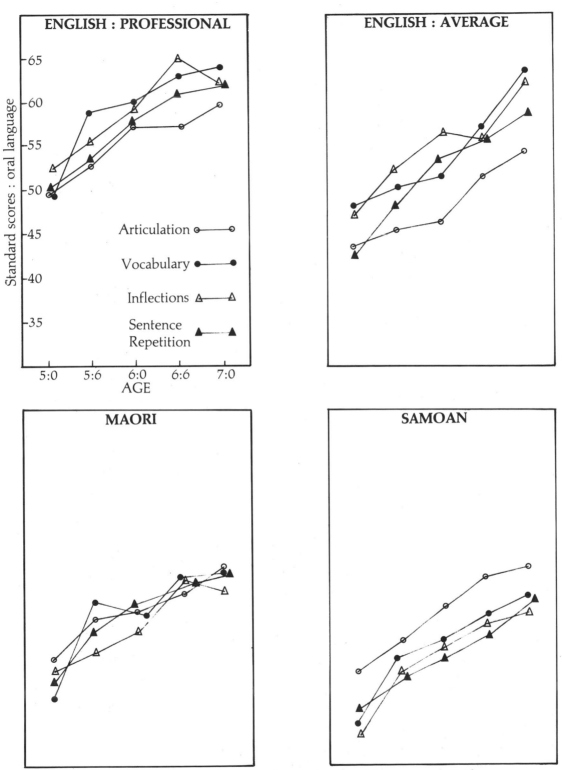

Figure 2: Change with age in four tests of oral language plotted for each language group in Sample A.

Table 3 — The Difficulty Order for Inflections for the Average English Group (N = 40)

	Type of Inflection					
No. of Errors	Plurals	3rd Pers. Sing. Verb Present	Verb: Simple Past	Present Participle	Future	Pronouns, Possessives, Adjectives
0 Easy Items	girls, hats	climb, sit fish, sweep wait, write	climb, fish wait, wash	climb, fish wash, wait write		mine, her you, his, them, dirty
2	gun-s					
3						father's
4	book-s	paint-s				
5	bik-s					
6	feet	open-s				
7	houses					
8	seaweed					their
9						old-est
10	climb-er					
11	wug-s		open-ed			
12		wash-es		open-ing		old-er
13		mot-s				happi-est
14		bod-s				
15	men				will naz	
16			sat		will sweep	
17			paint-ed		will paint	
18				bod-ding		himself
21	paint-er	naz-zes				
21	cal-ves					
25			swept			
26	gutch-es					
28						happi-er
29			wrote			
30			bod-ded			

Table 3 arranges the features tested in the difficulty order that was found for the Average English group. The left-hand column shows the number of errors made. Classes of words have been placed in separate columns across the table. The easy items are grouped at the top of the page and are not repeated in subsequent tables.

The plural phoneme /s/ or /z/ is relatively easy and so is the possessive *father's*. The present tense of the third person singular verb is also relatively easy, *paints, opens*; it requires only the addition of the same /s/ or /z/ phoneme. This rule can be generalised to nonsense words with relative ease, *bods, mots*.

The third way of forming the plural in English /əz/ in *houses* was more difficult and so was the phonologically similar verb form, *washes*. When children were required to apply these rules to nonsense nouns or verbs the items were amongst the most difficult in the test, *gutches, nazzes*.

The present participle and the simple past tense of regular verbs were easier to apply to real words, *opening, opened*, than to nonsense words, *bodding, bodded*. (The relative difficulty of *opened* and *opening* was the reverse of what would be expected from other research and this is perhaps due to a phonological feature of the word *opening*, the two unstressed syllables.) Two very difficult items are the irregular past tense verbs *wrote* and *swept*. The future tense was of moderate difficulty. The two pronoun items suggest a range of difficulty within this class of item. The superlative form of the adjective is easier than the comparative form.

Table 4 — The Difficulty Order for Inflections for the Maori Group (N = 40)						
Type of Inflection						
No. of Errors	Plurals	3rd Pers. Sing. Verbs Present	Verb: Simple Past	Present Participle	Future	Pronouns, Possessives, Adjectives
4	gun-s					
6	book-s					
8	bik-s					their
9						father's
13		paint-s				
14	seaweed	open-s	open-ed			
15				open-ing		
16	climb-er					old-est
18	feet	bod-s				
21	wug-s	mot-s		bod-ding	will paint	happi-est
22	houses				will naz	old-er
23	cal-ves		paint-ed			
23			sat			
27						himself
28					will sweep	
29	men	wash-es				
30	paint-er					
34						
35		naz-zes	wrote			happi-er
35			bod-ded			
36	gutch-es		swept			

The bilingual status of 75 percent of the Urban Samoan Group was established (Clay, 1971) so that a viable hypothesis would be that rules from the mother-tongue, Samoan, might create interference with the acquisition and use of English morphological rules and alter the difficulty sequence for Samoan children. The error scores of this group were very high but the order of difficulty is again similar to that of the Average English children (Table 5).

Table 5 — The Difficulty Order for Inflections for the Samoan Group (N = 40)						
	Type of Inflection					
No. of Errors	Plurals	3rd Pers. Sing. Verb Present	Verb: Simple Past	Present Participle	Future	Pronouns, Possessives, Adjectives
12	book-s					
14	gun-s					
15						their
17	seaweed		open-ed			
20						father's
21	climb-er	paint-s				old-est
22	feet					
23				open-ing	will naz	happi-est
24	bik-s					
25	houses	open-s	sat		will paint	old-er
26	paint-er			bod-ding		
27	wug-s	mot-s				himself
28		bod-s				
30			paint-ed		will sweep	
32	men					
32	cal-ves					
33						happi-er
35		wash-es				
37			wrote			
37		naz-zes	swept			
37			bod-ded			
38	gutch-es					

Development after seven years is reported by Presland (1973) who applied the same test to English, Maori, and Samoan children at 8:0, 9:0 and 10:0 years using 90 children from 12 Auckland schools. His mean scores showed an improvement with age for all three groups, with a fairly satisfactory level of scoring by the Urban Maori and Urban Samoan groups from 9:0 years onwards on the real word items. Yet at 10 years both the

Maori and Samoan mean scores were lower than those of the Average English children of 8 years; that is, an achievement lag still existed in this limited aspect of language development (Table 6).

	Clay			Presland		
Table 6 — Mean Inflection Test Scores in Clay and Presland Studies for Three Language Groups						
Age	5.0	6.0	7.0	8.0	9.0	10.0
Average English	19.6	21.9	29.6	32.9	33.3	35.0
Maori	9.8	14.9	23.2	22.1	28.3	28.6
Samoan	6.1	11.2	19.9	20.4	29.4	30.5

The items as arranged in Tables 3-5 cannot be interpreted as an order of acquisition because each table reports the pooled scores of children who were between 5 and 7 years. Whether the difficulty order reported is related to a difficulty sequence for acquisition would have to be tested on longitudinal data.

The four language groups had different degrees of control over the inflection rules of English, but within each group the patterns of difficulties were similar. They appear to be determined more by factors within the English language, such as frequency, regularity or phonemic shape, than by factors within the children such as interference from features or rules of another dialect or language.

None of the groups showed particular and different patterns of responding but this does not in itself imply that special instruction was not needed. What it does suggest is that a similar teaching sequence might apply to many language groups. One research study (Osser, Wang and Zaid, 1969) suggests a procedure for achieving effective learning with inflections. While intuitive judgement might lead teachers to go from the singular to the plural, or uninflected to inflected, or present to past the Osser et al research presents strong evidence that for the best results the teacher's examples should be the 'hard' one or inflected example and the child's response the 'easier' of the two paired items, the uninflected example.

Descriptive research of this kind can yield important information about regularities in acquisition. Such data is helpful for teachers in understanding what a child can already do. Seeing a particular child's achievement in the context of what we know about the general patterns of acquisition can assist teachers in deciding what to emphasise next in a learning programme.

Appendix — Construction of the Test

After preliminary trials the following 62 items were used in a pilot study with 40 children from several ethnic groups in Auckland in 1962.

Plurals	Regular	*girls*	guns	wugs	
		hats	books	biks	
		houses	*pouches*(x)	gutches	
	Irregular	men	feet	calves	
	Uninflected	seaweed	*hay*		
Possessive	Nouns and	*girl's*	father's	their	
	Pronouns	*his*	her	*mine*	
Pronouns		*you*	*them*	himself	
Noun Agent		painter	climber		
Adjectives		*dirtier*	*dirtiest*		
		happier	happiest		
		older	oldest		
		kwerkier(x)	*kwerkiest*(x)		
Verbs		*fishing*	*washing*	*writing*	*waiting*
		climbing	opening	bodding	
		climbs	*sits*	*fishes*	
		opens	paints	washes	
		mots	bods	nazzes	
		climbed	*fished*	*waited*	
		washed	opened	painted	bodded
		sat	swept	wrote	
		will paint	will sweep	will naz	

Items were discarded because
- several fell at the same difficulty level
- some were easy items which most children answered correctly (in italics above)
- some were difficult items for almost all children (in italics followed by x)

Biks and Gutches — References

BERKO, JEAN The child's learning of English morphology, *Word*, 14, 150-77, 1958.

CLAY, MARIE M. Language skills: a comparison of Maori, Samoan and Pakeha children aged five to seven years, *New Zealand Journal of Educational Studies*, 5:2, 153-62, 1970.

CLAY, MARIE M. The Polynesian language skills of Maori and Samoan school entrants, *International Journal of Psychology*, 6:2, 135-45, 1971.

CLAY, MARIE M. The development of morphological rules in children of differing language backgrounds, *New Zealand Journal of Educational Studies*, 9:2, 113-121, 1974.

CLAY, MARIE M. Learning to inflect English words, *Regional English Language Centre Journal*, 6, 11, 33-42, 1975.

DALE, P. S. *Language Development: Structure and Function*. Hinsdale, Illinois: The Dryden Press, 1972.

KIRK, S. A. and McCARTHY, J. J. The Illinois Test of Psycholinguistic Abilities, *Amer. J. Defic.*, 399-412, 1966.

OSSER, H., WANG, M. D. and ZAID, F. The young child's ability to imitate and comprehend speech: a comparison of two sub-cultural groups, *Child Development*, 40, 1063-75, 1969.

PRESLAND, I. V. Inflection skills: a comparison between Maori, Samoan and English children aged eight to ten years, Unpubl. Dip.Ed. Thesis, University of Auckland Library, 1973.

SELBY, S. The development of morphological rules in children, *Brit. J. Educ. Psychology*, 42:5, 293-9, 1972.